Contents

Preface 5

Introduction 6

As She is Spoke — Short Version 9

As She is Spoke — Long Version 11

As She is Spoke — Translation 14

Story One — Short Version 16

Story One — Long Version 17

Story One — Translation 18

Story Two — Short Version 19

Story Two — Long Version 20

Story Two — Translation 21

A poem 22

GLOSSARY :

Cockney — English 23

English — Cockney 44

A Few Indelicacies 63

UP THE FROG

FROG

The road to Cockney Rhyming Slang

by Sydney (Steak) T. Kendall

WOLFE PUBLISHING LTD
10 EARLHAM STREET LONDON WC2

To **Christopher**
as part of his
education

SBN 72340138 1 X
© Sydney T. Kendall 1969
© Wolfe Publishing Ltd. 1969

Preface

There is nothing pretentious about this Glossary. I have not tried to delve deeply into the whys and wherefores of Rhyming Slang but have compiled an alphabetical collation of words which have been in use to my knowledge, for over sixty years, by my own 'townies'.

Born in London (but not within sound of St. Mary-le-Bow church bells, even with the wind in the right direction), I have had the great pleasure of knowing Cockneys since I was a boy. I was very soon picking up Rhyming Slang expressions from them.

As a boy soprano on the halls I learned a lot from fellow artistes (much older than myself) and was always showing off my 'knowledge'. In this way I began to collect Rhyming Slang phrases.

Between the wars I found Rhyming Slang not used so very much. World War II seemed to bring it to life again (The Great War had had the same effect).

This book is an attempt to put on record some of the words and appropriate phrases I have accumulated over the years. I hope you enjoy it – and use it.

'Steak' **T. Kendall**

Introduction

SLANG – just plain slang – is described as 'a conventional tongue with many dialects, which are, as a rule, unintelligible to outsiders . . . any kind of colloquial and familiar language serving as a kind of class or professional shibboleth'.

This Glossary has been compiled to assist the uninitiated in the use of a different kind of slang which, to quote the above description, is, as a rule, 'unintelligible to outsiders'. Rhyming Slang is said to have originated in the underworld of London around the middle of the nineteenth century; to have been used by thieves and vagabonds.

There is no doubt that these 'gentry' created this language to outwit the inquisitive 'eavesdropper' or even the police of that day. Rhyming slang was (and still is) a humorous and light-hearted form of expression. There is no greater exponent of rhyming slang than the 'Cockney'. To be with Cockneys, whether in the markets or in their favourite pub, is an amusing and enlightening experience.

It has always been understood that a true Cockney is born within the sound of the bells of St. Mary-le-Bow Church; this is still so today. Every Londoner cannot be a cockney, but the cockney accent is immediately recognisable. A visit to the markets of the metropolis (Covent Garden, Spitalfields, Billingsgate, etc.), will give the visitor to London an opportunity of hearing Cockney slang 'as she is spoke'.

Many people have the impression that the Cockney and the Coster are one and the same. This is not so, the latter are the 'barrow boys' of today and have a peculiar slang of their own. They often use 'back-slang', wherein words are, more or less, spelt backwards. Thus, a Smithfield porter can be heard asking for a 'gel o' kayrop', when what he really wants is a leg of pork. The use of back-slang is now waning.

The finest exponent of Cockney accent was Albert Chevalier, the famous Music Hall artist. His *My Old Dutch, I'll be as right as Ninepence, Knocked 'Em in the Old Kent Road*, were classical examples. His recordings speak for themselves and demonstrate the lack of aspirates and change of vowel pronunciations.

Rhyming slang usually takes the form of two

or three words, the last of which rhymes with the original word, thus 'stairs' becomes 'apples and pears', and 'collar' – ''oller boys 'oller'. In many instances the slang is shortened to the first word only, as in 'taters in the mould' (cold), becomes simply 'taters'. This shortened version is used considerably (in conversation) and is, to say the least, very misleading to a stranger. It is difficult to associate a 'tumble' with a drink. Nevertheless a drink *is* a 'tumble down the sink'.

As She Is Spoke —
Short Version

1. Up the *apples* to *lemon* me *Ramsgates*.

2. Take the *cherry* for a *ball* up the *frog*.

3. 'Ave a *butcher's* at *Steak*, 'es *elephant's!*

4. Old *oats* 'as got a lovely *Conan* on 'is *bushel*.

5. Let's go on the *river* and get *elephant's!*

6. Will you *sausage* a *goose's* for me?

7. Don't I get no *kitchen* then?

8. 'Taint 'arf *taters* in 'ere!

9. I'm takin' me *ima* orf, its proper *peas* 'ere.

10. 'Es in a proper *two 'n' eight*, 'es lorst 'is *'ampsteads*.

11. Lend us *'arf 'n* Oxford, I'm *boracic!*

12. Two drops of *pimple* and a drop o' *needle* for the *struggle*.

13. That's a decent pair of *turtles* you've got!

14. She 'ad a skirt near up to her *fife*, but a lovely pair of *scotches*.

15. Shan't be a *cock* – just goin' for a *Jimmy*.

16. Two weeks behind with the *duke* and I ain't got no *bees*.

17. I 'ad nine pints o' *pig's* an' that's a fair *tumble*.

18. I've bin in the ol' *Uncle* for a couple o' weeks with a touch o' *salmon*.

19. 'is *plates pen and ink*. 'Is *almonds* must be *reels*.

20. I've asked the *baked* for a *Joe* an' some *rosebuds*.

21. This 'ere bloke grabs 'im by the *'oller boys* an' gives 'im a real four'pn'y in the *Newington's*.

22. Shove this *saucepan* in yer *sky*.

23. You'd 'ardly *Adam* it – 'is trouble's goin' to 'ave anvver *Gawdfer!*

24. D'yer want any *fisherman's* wiv yer *pimple?*

25. Bung it in the *Johnnie* 'longside the *dickory*.

26. She 'ad golden *barnet* an' a smashin' pair of *minces*.

27. 'E's only got one *mince* and 'e's as *mutt'n* as anyfink.

28. I got this *Gordon* orf of a *five to*.

29. My *skin* 'as got a new *artful*. I reckon 'es a *King*.

30. Shut yer *North*, yer a *Dunlop*.

31. I've got to take the *cocksparrer* up the *Dolly* fer some *roses*.

32. 'E wraps the *Lilian* in some *linen* 'n' orf I *scarper*.

33.   'E said 'e was the *damager* an' give me 'is *Wilkie.*

34.   I got 'im right on the *Gunga* with me *Oliver* an' put 'im to *Bo-Peep.*

35.   The ol' *currant* was a-shinin' through the *burnt.*

As She Is Spoke —
Long Version

1.   Up the *apples and pears* to *lemon squash* me *Ramsgate Sands.*

2.   Take the *cherry 'og* for a *ball o' chalk* up the *frog and toad.*

3.   'Ave a *butcher's 'ook* at *Steak and Kidney,* 'e's *elephant's trunk!*

4.   Old *oats and barley* 'as got a lovely *Conan Doyle* on the back of 'is *bushel and peck.*

5.   Let's go on the *River Ouse* and get *elephant's trunk.*

6.   Will yer *sausage and mash* a *goose's neck* for me?

7.   Don't I get no *kitchen range* then?

8.   T'ain't arf *taters in the mould* in 'ere!

9.   I'm takin' me *I'm afloat* orf, its proper *peas in the pot* in 'ere.

10.   'es in a proper *two an' eight* – 'es lorst 'is *'ampstead 'eath.*

11. Lend us 'arf an *Oxford scholar*, I'm *boracic lint*.

12. Two drops of *pimple and blotch* and a *needle and pin* for the *struggle and strife*.

13. That's a decent pair of *turtle doves* you've got!

14. She 'ad a skirt up to her *fife 'n' drum*, but a lovely pair of *scotch pegs*.

15. Shan't be a *cock linnet* – just going for a *Jimmy Riddle*.

16. Two weeks be'ind wiv the *Duke o' Kent* an' I ain't got no *bees 'n' oney*.

17. I 'ad nine pints of *pig's ear* an' that's a fair *tumble dahn the sink*.

18. I've bin in the 'ole *Uncle Ned* for a couple o' weeks wiv a touch of the *salmon trout*.

19. 'is *plates o' meat pen and ink*. 'Is *almond rocks* must be *reels of cotton*.

20. I've asked the *baked potato* for a *Joe Blake* and some *rosebuds*.

21. This 'ere bloke grabs 'im by the *'oller boys 'oller* and gives 'im a real *fourpenny* one in the *Newington Butts*.

22. Shove this *saucepan lid* in yer *sky rocket*.

23. You'd 'ardly *Adam 'n' Eve* it – 'is *trouble and strife's* goin' to 'ave anuvver *Gawd forbid*.

24. D'yer want any *fisherman's daughter* wiv yer *pimple and blotch?*

25. Bung it in the *Johnnie 'Orner* alongside the *dickory dock.*

26. She 'ad golden *Barnet Fair* an' a smashin' pair of *mince pies.*

27. 'E's only got one *mince pie* and 'e's as *Mutt an' Jeff* as anyfink.

28. I got this *Gordon 'n' Gotch* from a *five to two.*

29. My *skin and blister* 'as a new *Artful Dodger* – I reckon he's a *King Lear.*

30. Shut yer *North 'n' South* – yer a *Dunlop tyre.*

31. I've got to take the *cock sparrer* up the *Dolly Varden* fer some *rosebuds.*

32. 'E wraps the *Lilian Gish* in some *linen draper* an orf I *scapa flow.*

33. 'E said 'e was the *damager* an' give me 'is *Wilkie Bard.*

34. I got 'im right on the *Gunga Din* with me *Oliver Twist* an' put 'im to *Bo-Peep.*

35. The ol' *currant bun* was a-shinin' through the *burnt cinder.*

As She Is Spoke —
Translation

1. Up *stairs* to *wash* my *hands*.
2. Take the *dog* for a *walk* up the *road*.
3. Have a look at *Sydney*, he's *drunk!*
4. Old *Charley* has got a lovely *boil* on the back of his *neck*.
5. Let's go on the *booze* and get *drunk*.
6. Will you *cash* a *cheque* for me?
7. Don't I get any *change* then?
8. It isn't half *cold* in here!
9. I'm taking my *coat* off, it's proper *hot* in here!
10. He's in a proper *state* – he's lost his *teeth!*
11. Lend me a *half-a-crown*, I'm *skint*.
12. Two drops of *Scotch* and a *gin* for the *wife*.
13. That's a decent pair of *gloves* you've got!
14. She had a skirt up to her *bum* but a lovely pair of *legs*.
15. Shan't be a *minute* – just going to have a *piddle*.
16. Two weeks behind with the *rent* and I haven't any *money*.
17. I had nine pints of *beer* and that's a fair *drink*.

18. I've been in the old *bed* for a couple of weeks with a touch of *gout*.

19. His *feet stink* – his *socks* must be *rotten*.

20. I have asked the *waiter* for a *steak* and some *potatoes*.

21. This here bloke grabs him by the *collar* and gives him a real *fourpenny one* in the *guts*.

22. Shove this *quid* in your *pocket*.

23. You would hardly *believe* it – his *wife* is going to have another *kid*.

24. Do you want any *water* with your *Scotch?*

25. Bung it in the *corner* alongside the *clock*.

26. She had golden *hair* and a smashing pair of *eyes*.

27. He has only got one *eye* and he is as *deaf* as anything.

28. I got this *watch* from a *Jew*.

29. My *sister* has got a new *lodger* – I reckon he is a *queer*.

30. Shut your *mouth* – you are a *liar*.

31. I have to take the *barrow* up to *Covent Garden* for some *potatoes*.

32. He wraps the *fish* in some *paper* and off I *go*.

33. He said he was the *manager* and gave me his *card*.

34. I got him right on the *chin* with my *fist* and put him to *sleep*.

35. The old *sun* was shining through the *window*.

Story One — Short Version

I WAS taking the *cherry* for a *ball* up the *frog* the other night, when I met a *china* o' mine. We 'ad a few *dickies* an' then he suggested we 'ad a *tumble* together.

Well, instead of going into the Red Lion, we went into the first *rub-a* we comes to.

I sez 'Wot are you going to 'ave?' 'E sez, 'I'll have a drop of *pig's*', so I gets a pint o' *pig's* fer 'im an' I 'ad a drop of *needle*, just fer a start.

We got chattin' and one fing led to anuvver, when we 'ears the Guv'nor calling 'Time gents, please!'

I could 'ardly *Adam* it that we'd bin at it so long. So I gets an *'arris* of *in-an'-out* for the *plates*, picks up the *cherry* an' orf we *scarpa*.

As its so *'Arry* I gets on a *trouble* an' when I gets 'ome I find the *plates* is out 'aving a *butcher's* round the *rub-as* for me and the *cherry*. So I gets up the *apples* an' into the ol' *uncle* and when she comes in, there I am wiv me *loaf* on the *weepin'*, readin' the *linen*.

She starts a few *earlies* but I don't want no

bull, so I turns over an' in a couple of *cocks* I'm
Bo-Peep.

Story One — Long Version

I WAS taking the *cherry 'og*, for a *ball o' chalk*, up
the *frog and toad* the other night, when I met a
china plate o' mine. We 'ad a few *dicky birds* an'
then 'e suggested we 'ad a *tumble dahn the sink*
together.

Well, instead of going into the Red Lion, we
went into the first *rub-a-dub* we comes to. I sez
'what are you going to 'ave?' 'E sez, 'I'll 'ave a
drop o' *pig's ear*, so I gets a pint o' *pig's ear* for
'im an' I 'ad a drop of *needle and pin*, just for a
start.

We got chatting an' one fing led to anuvver
when we 'ears the Guv'nor calling 'Time, gents
please!'

I could 'ardly *Adam and Eve* it that we 'ad bin
at it so long. So I gets an *Aristotle* of *In-and-out*
for the *plates and dishes*, picks up the *cherry 'og* an'
orf we *Scarpa Flow*.

As its so *'Arry Tate* I gets on a *trouble an' fuss*,
an' when I gets 'ome, I find the *plates 'n' dishes* is
out 'avin' a *butchers 'ook* round the *rub-a-dubs* for
me and the *cherry 'og*. So I gets up the *apples and
pears* an' into the ol' *uncle Ned* and when she
comes in, there I am wiv' me *loaf o' bread* on the

weeping willow, readin' the *linen draper*. She starts a few *early birds* but I don't want no *bull & cow*, so I turns over an' in a couple o' *cock linnets* I'm *Bo-Peep*.

Story One — Translation

I WAS taking the *dog* for a *walk* up the *road* the other night, when I met a *mate* of mine. We had a few *words* and then he suggested we had a *drink* together.

Well, instead of going into the 'Red Lion', we went into the first *pub* we came to.

I said, 'what are you going to have?' He said 'I'll have a drop of *beer*', so, I got a pint of *beer* for him and I had a drop of *gin*, for a start.

We got chatting and one thing led to another, when we hear the Landlord calling 'Time, Gents please'.

I could hardly *believe* that we had been at it for so long, so I got a *bottle* of *stout* for the *missus*, picked up the *dog* and off we go.

As it's so *late* I got on a *bus* and when I got home, I found the *missus* is out having a *look* round the *pubs* for me and the *dog*. So I got *upstairs* and into *bed*, and when she came in, there I was with my *head* on the *pillow*, reading the *paper*.

She started having a few *words* but I didn't want a *row*, so I turned over, and in a couple of *minutes* I was *asleep*.

Story Two — Short Version

MY *one 'n' t'other* 'as bought 'isself a new lot of gear. 'E must be in the *bees* 'cos 'e's got a new *ima*, a new *whistle* wiv a *Peckham* to go wiv it an' a new fancy *Jim Prescott*. Then 'e's got a pair of yellow *turtles* on his *Ramsgates* to stop 'em getting *taters*, an' on top of this lot there's a new *titfer*. I told him 'e looked a proper *oats*.

'E sez, 'This ain't all I got. Wot abaht me new *Dicky* wiv the *'oller boys* to match, like?' He hitches up his *round me's* and shows orf his new pair of *almonds* an' a posh pair of *daisies*. On his *Chalk* is a *Cousin Ella*. 'In case it starts to *France*', 'e sez.

'E offered me one of his *Harrys*, but I sees 'e' as a *Spanish* on isself. 'I've got a *birch* rahn the *Johnnie*,' 'e sez. 'Come in an 'ave a drop o' *pimple*.'

So I goes along wiv 'im an' 'e gets aht a *Jennie* an' in we goes into this 'ere *birch* 'es got.

You oughter seen it! There was everythink in it! – a *Cain* wiv three *Scotches*, a *la-di* over on one side wiv all the *tumbles* you could think of; three *Owens* wiv *chalks* an' all, an' a 'lectric *dickory* on the mantelpiece over the *Jeremiah*.

'E'd got a *Nervo* in the *burnt* and to top the lot a flippin' *Joanna*! 'N' 'es only the *Artful*! I bet that little lot costs 'im a packet – then 'es got the *Duke* on top of that lot! Cor! 'E must be rollin' in it!

Story Two — Long Version

My *one 'n' t'other* 'as bought 'isself a new lot of gear. 'E must be in the *'bees 'n' honey'* c'os 'es got a new *I'm afloat*, a new *whistle 'n' flute* wiv a *Peckham Rye* to go wiv it an' a fancy new *Jim Prescott*. Then 'es got a pair of yeller *turtle doves* on 'is *Ramsgate Sands* to stop 'em getting *taters in the mould*, an' on top of this lot there's a new *tit-fer-tat*, I told 'im he looked a proper *oats 'n' barley*.

'E sez 'This ain't all I got. Wot abaht me new *dicky dirt* wiv the *oller boys oller* to match, like? 'E 'itches up his *round the 'ouses* an' shows orf 'is new pair of *almond rocks* an' a posh pair o' *daisy roots*. On 'is *Chalk Farm* is a *Cousin Ella*. 'In case it starts to *France an' Spain*,' 'e sez. 'E offers me one of 'is *Harry Wraggs*, but I sees 'e' as a *Spanish Guitar* on isself.

'I've got a *birch broom* rahn the *Johnnie 'Orner*,' 'e sez. 'Come in 'an 'ave a drop o' *pimple and blotch*.

So I goes along wiv 'im an' 'e gets aht a *Jennie Lee* an' in we goes into this 'ere *birch broom* 'es got.

You orta seen it! There was everythink in it – a *Cain 'n' Able* wiv three *Scotch pegs* on it, a *la-di-da* over on one side wiv all the *tumble-dahn the sink* you could think of; Three *Owen Nares* wiv *Chalk Farms* 'n'all 'n' a 'lectric *Dickory Dock* on the mantelpiece over the *Jeremiah*.

'E'd got a *Nervo & Knox* in the *burnt cinder*, 'n' to top the lot a flippin' *Joanna*! 'N' 'e's only the *Artful Dodger*! I bet that little lot costs 'im a packet – then 'e's got the *Duke o' Kent* on top o' that lot! Cor! 'E must be rollin' in it!

Story Two — Translation

MY *brother* has bought himself a lot of new gear. He must be in the *money* because he has got a new *coat*, a new *suit* with a *tie* to go with it, and a fancy new *waistcoat*. Then he has got a pair of yellow *gloves* on his *hands* to stop them getting *cold*, and, on top of this lot there is a new *hat*. I told him he looked a proper *Charlie*.

He said, 'This is not all I have got. What about my new *shirt* with the *collar* to match'? He hitched up his *trousers* and showed off his new pair of *socks*, and a posh pair of *boots*. On his *arm* was an *umbrella*. 'In case it starts to *rain*,' he said.

He offered me one of his *cigarettes* (*fags*), but I noticed he was smoking a *cigar* himself.

'I've a *room* round the *corner*,' he said. 'Come in and have a drop of *Scotch*'.

So I went along with him and he got out a *key* and in we went into this *room* he has. You should have seen it! There was everything in it –

a *table* with three *legs* on it, *a bar* over on one side
with all the *drinks* you could think of; three
chairs with *arms*, too, and an electric *clock* on the
mantlepiece over the *fire*. He had a *television set*
(*box*) in the *window* and, to top everything, a
flipping *piano*! And he's only the *lodger*!

I bet that little lot costs him a packet – then
he has the *rent* on top of that lot, Cor! He must
be rolling in it!

A Poem

I was sitting in front of the *Jeremiah*
A-warming me *plates of meat*
When there comes a knock at the *Rory O' More*
That made me *raspberry tart* beat.

I opened the *Rory* and standing there
Was me *one 'n' t'other* called Ted.
'E says 'I'm back from Australia.'
Says I 'we thought you was *brahn bread*'.

'E looked at me wiv 'is one *mince pie*
'Is *Jem Mace* 'ad a nasty grin
I thought to meself – "Es *elephant's trunk,*
I don't dare let 'im in'.

'It's Ted (or his *pillar and post*)' I cried
In a proper *two and eight*
So I slammed the *Rory O' More* in 'is *Jem*
An' left 'im to 'is fate.

Glossary

Cockney — English

A

Adam & Eve	Believe
Airs & graces	{Braces Epsom Races Faces
Alligator	Later
Almond rocks	Socks
Alphonse	Ponce (alt)
'Ampstead 'Eath	Teeth
Anna Maria	Fire
Apple fritter	Bitter (Beer)
Apple pie	Sky
Apples & pears	Stairs
Apples & rice	Nice
'Appy 'arf hours	Flowers
April fool	Stool
April fools	{Stools Tools Pools (gambling)
April showers	Flowers

'Arf 'n Oxford scholar	Half dollar (*2/6*d)
'Arf inch	Pinch (steal)
Army 'n' Navy	Gravy
'Arry Randell	Candle
'Arry Tate	Late State (nervous) Plate
'Arry Wragg	Fag (cigarette)
Artful Dodger	Lodger

B

Baa-lamb	Tram (alt)
Babbling brook	Cook Crook
Baked potato (pron. potater)	Waiter
Baker's dozen	Cousin
Ball 'o chalk	Walk
Balloon	Saloon (bar) (alt)
Band of 'Ope	Soap (alt)
Barnaby Rudge	Judge
Barnet Fair	Hair
Bat 'n' Wicket	Ticket
Bath bun	Son Sun

Battle cruiser	Boozer (pub)
Bazaar	Bar (pub)
Becher's Brook	Look
Beehive	Five (£5)
Beecham's pill	Bill (account)
Beef 'n' mutton	Glutton
Bees 'n' honey	Money
Billy Button	Mutton
Birch broom	Room
Bird lime	Time
Bite(s) & scratch (es)	Match (es)
Black man kissed 'er	Sister
Bladder o' lard	Card
Blue Moon	Spoon
Bo-peep	Sleep
Boracic lint	Skint (stony broke)
Borrow 'n' beg	Egg
Bows 'n' arrows	Sparrows
(pron. arrers)	(pron. sparrers)
Box o' tricks	Flicks (the cinema)
Brahn bread	Dead
Brass tacks	Facts
Bread 'n' butter	Gutter

Bread 'n' cheese	Sneeze
Bread 'n' jam	Tram (alt)
Brewer's bung	Tongue
Bride 'n' groom	Broom
Bright 'n' frisky	Whisky
Brussels sprout	Boy Scout
Buckle me shoe	Jew (alt)
Buck's Hussar	Cigar (alt)
Bull 'n' cow	Row (an altercation)
Bullock's horn	Pawn
Burnt cinder	Window (pron. winder)
Burton-on-Trent	Rent
Bushel 'n' peck	neck
Bushey Park	Lark
Butcher's 'ook	Look

C

Cain 'n' Abel	Table
Canal boat	Tote (totalisator)
Canoes	Shoes

Cape o' Good 'Ope	Soap
Cape 'Orn	Dawn
Captain Cook	Book
Cash 'n' carried	Married
Cat 'n' mouse	House
Cat's milk	Silk
Cellar flap	Tap (dance)
Chalk Farm	Arm
Charing Cross (pron. Crorse)	Horse
Charley Dilk	Milk
Charley Mason	Basin
Cherry 'og	Dog
Cherries (the) (cherry 'ogs)	Dog Racing
Cherry Ripe	Pipe (smoker's)
Chevy Chase	Face
China plate	Mate
Chop sticks	Six (Bingo)
Christmas cards	Guards (the) (military)
Clever Mike	Bike (bicycle)
Clicketty Click	Sixty six (Bingo)
Clod 'opper	Copper (Policeman)

Coals 'n' Coke	Broke (financially)
Coat 'n' Badge (Doggett's)	Cadge
Cock 'n' hen	{Pen Ten pounds (£10)
Cock linnet	Minute (time)
Cockroach	Coach
Cock sparrow (pron. sparrer)	Barrow (pron. barrer)
Cocoa	Say so
Cold potato (pron. potater)	Waiter (alt)
Conan Doyle	Boil
Corns 'n' bunions	Onions
Cough 'n' sneeze	Cheese
Country cousin	Dozen
Cousin Ella	Umbrella
Covent Garden	Farthing (pron. farden)
Cow 'n' calf	Laugh (pron. larf)
Cuddle & kiss	Miss (a girl)
Currant bun	{Son Sun
Custard 'n' jelly	Telly (TV set)

Cut & carried	Married (alt)

D

Cut & carried	Married (alt)
Daffadown-dilly	Silly (alt)
Daisy Dormer	Warmer
Daisy roots	Boots
Damager (Damaging Director)	Manager
Darby 'n' Joan	Phone
Day's a dawning	Morning
Derby Brights	Lights
Derby Kelly	Belly
Derry 'n' Toms	Bombs
Dickory dock	Clock
Dicky bird	Word
Dicky dirt	Shirt
Dig in the grave	Shave
Ding dong	Song
Dinky-do	Twenty two (Bingo)
Dirty tyke	Bike (bicycle)
Dog 'n' cat	Mat
Dolly Varden	Farthing (pron. farden) Garden

Dover Harbour — Barber

Dripping toast — Host

Drum 'n' fife — Knife

Duke of Argyll — File (a) (tool)

Duke o' Kent — Rent

Duke o' York — Fork / Pork

Dunlop tyre — Liar

E

Early bird — Word

Early hours — Flowers

East 'n' West — Vest

Eighteen pence — Sense

Elephant's trunk — Drunk

Epsom Races — Braces / Faces

Everton toffee — Coffee

Eyes o' blue — True

F

Farmer Giles — Piles (Haemorrhoids)

Feather 'n' flip — Kip (bed or sleep)

Field o' wheat	Street
Fife 'n' drum	Bum (buttocks)
Fine 'n' dandy	Brandy
Finger 'n' thumb	Rum
Fisherman's daughter	Water
Five to two	Jew (alt)
Four by two	Jew (alt)
France 'n' Spain	Rain
Frog 'n' toad	Road

G

Game o' nap	Cap (headgear)
Garden gate	Magistrate
Garden gates	Rates
Gawd (God) forbid	Kid (a child) / Lid (a hat)
Gay 'n' frisky	Whisky
German bands	Hands
Gert 'n' Daisy	Lazy
Gertie Gitana	Banana
Ginger Beer	Engineer
Girl 'n' boy	Saveloy (sausage)

Give-a-guck	{ Cook
(pron. gook)	{ Look
Give 'n' take	Cake (alt)
Gold watch	Scotch (whisky)
Goose's neck	Cheque
Gordon 'n' Gotch	Watch (timepiece)
Grass 'opper	Copper (policeman)
Greengage	Stage (theatre)
Greengages	Wages
Grey mare	Fare (bus or train)
Gunga din	Chin
Grumble & mutter	Flutter (a bet)
Guzunter (goes under)	Punter (racing)

H

Hackney marsh	Glass (drinking)
Half past two	Jew (alt)
Harvey Nicholls	Pickles
Hearts of Oak	Broke (financially)
Hedge 'n' ditch	Pitch (cricket)
Here 'n' there	Chair (alt)
Herman Fink	Ink

Hi-diddle-diddle	{Middle {Fiddle
High stepper	Pepper
Hobbledy 'oy	Boy
Hobson's choice	Voice
Holy Friar	Liar
Holy Ghost	{Host {Toast (bread) {Winning Post (racecourse)
Horses 'n' carts	Darts
Horse 'n' trough	Cough

I

I suppose	Nose
I'm afloat	Coat
In 'n' out	Stout (beverage)
Iron horse	Toss (pron. torse) up
Irish stew	True
Isle o' Wight	Tight (tipsy)

J

| Jack 'n' Jill | {Bill (account)
{Till (cash)
{Hill |

Jack the Dandy	{Brandy {Randy
Jack tar	Half a bar (ten shillings)
Jack Jones	Alone
Jack the Ripper	Kipper
Jam jar	Car
Jem Mace	Face
Jenny Lee	Key
Jeremiah	Fire
Jim Skinner	Dinner
Jim Prescott	Waistcoat
(pron. Preskit)	(pron. Weskit)
Jimmy O'Goblin	Sovereign (pron. Sovrin) ($£1$)
Jimmy Riddle	Piddle (urinate)
Jitter	Gin & bitter (mixed) (dog's nose)
Joe Blake	Steak
Joe Tank	Bank
Joanna	Piano (pron. pianna)
Johnny 'Orner	Corner

K

Kidney Punch	Lunch
Kilkenny	Penny
King Lear	Ear
Kitchen Range	Change (£ s d)

L

La-di-da	Car
Lady Godiva	Fiver (£5 note)
Last card in the pack	Sack (dismissal)
Laugh 'n' joke	Smoke
Lean 'n' lurch	Church
Lemon squash	Wash
Light 'n' dark	Park
Lilian Gish	Fish
Linen draper	Newspaper / Paper
Lion's share	Chair (alt)
Loaf o' bread	Head
Lollipop	Shop
Londonderry	Sherry
Long(s) & Linger(s)	Finger(s)

Long Acre	Baker
Loop the loop	Soup
Lord Lovell	Shovel
Lord Mayor	Swear
Lord o' the Manor	Tanner (6d piece)
Love one another	{ Brother / Mother
Lucy Locket	Pocket

M

Macaroni (a)	Pony (£25)
Mahatma Gandhi	Shandy
Marie Correlli	Telly (TV set)
Me 'n' you	Menu
Merry old soul	Hole
Mince pie(s)	Eye(s)
Molly Malone	Phone
Molly O'Morgan	Organ
Mother 'Ubbard	Cupboard
Mozzle 'n' brocha (Yiddish)	On the knocker (door to door salesman)
Mrs. Duckett	Bucket
Mum 'n' Dad	Mad
Mums 'n' Dads	Pads (cricket)

Mutt 'n' Jeff   Deaf

N

Nanny goat	Tote (totalisator)
Near 'n' far	Bar (pub)
Needle 'n' pin	Gin
Needle 'n' thread	Bread
Nervo 'n' Knox	Goggle Box (TV set)
Newington Butts	Guts
Noah's ark	{ Park Nark (informer)
North 'n' South	Mouth

O

Oats 'n' barley	Charlie
Oliver Twist	Fist
'Oller boys 'oller	Collar
One 'n t'other	{ Brother Mother
Oscar Asche	Cash (alt)
Overcoat maker	Undertaker
'Ow d'yer do	Stew
Owen Nares	Chairs

| Oxford scholar | Dollar |

P

P's 'n' Q's	Shoes
Pair o' braces	Races
Pair o' kippers	Slippers
Peas in the pot	Hot
Peckham Rye	Tie
Pen 'n' ink	Stink
Penny bun	{ Son Sun
Photo-finish	Guinness (stout)
Piccadilly	Silly
Pickled pork	Chalk
Pig's ear	Beer
Pillar 'n' post	Ghost
Pimple 'n' blotch	Scotch (whisky)
Pipe yer eye	Cry
Pitch 'n' toss	Boss
Plate of 'am	Tram (alt.)
Plates 'n' dishes	Missus (the wife)
Plates o' meat	Feet

Pope o' Rome	Home
Pork pie	Lie (untruth)
Pot 'n' pan	Old man (father)
Put 'n' take	Cake

R

Ramsgate Sands	Hands
Raspberry tart	Heart
Rats 'n' mice	Dice
Read 'n' write	Fight
Reels o' cotton	Rotten
Rhubarb (pron. rubub)	Sub. (on a/c wages)
Richard the Third	Bird
Rise 'n' shine	Wine
River Ouse	Booze
Rock of ages	Wages
Roll me in the gutter	Butter
Rookery Nook	{ Book { Cook
Rory O'More	{ Door { Floor
Rosebuds	Spuds (potatoes)
Rosy Lee	Tea
Rotten row	Blow

Round the 'ouses	Trousers
Rub-a-dub	Pub

S

Salmon trout	Gout
Sarah Gamp	Lamp
Saucepan lid	Kid (child) / Quid (£1)
Sausage & mash	Cash (alt)
Scapa Flow	Go!
Scotch pegs	Legs
Sexton Blake	Cake
Sinbad the Sailor	Tailor
Sit beside 'er	Cider
Skin 'n' blister	Sister
Skip 'n' jump	Pump
Sky rocket	Pocket
Skyscraper	Newspaper
Smile & titter	Mild & bitter (mixed beer)
Song o' the thrush	Brush
Sorry 'n' sad	Bad
Spanish guitar	Cigar
Spanish Main	Drain
Spanish onion	Bunion

Sprazey Anna	Tanner (*6*d piece)
Stammer 'n' stutter	Butter
Stand at ease	Cheese
Steak 'n' kidney	Sydney
Steam tug	{Mug {Bug
Struggle 'n' strain	Train
Sweeney Todd	Flying Squad (police)

T

'Taters in the mould	Cold
Tea 'n' cocoa	Say so
Tea leaf	Thief
Teddy bears	Pears
These 'n' those	Toes
Thomas Tilling	Shilling (piece)
Three blind mice	Rice
Tiddley-wink(s)	Drink(s)
Tin tack	Sack (dismissal)
Tit fer tat	Hat
Tod Sloane	Alone
Tomfoolery	Jewellery
Tom Thumb	{Rum {Bum (buttocks)

Tommy Tupper	Supper
Trouble 'n' fuss	Bus
Trouble 'n' strife	Wife
Tumble dahn the sink	Drink
Turpentine (shortened to 'turps')	Serpentine (Kensington Gardens) ('Serps')
Turtle doves	Gloves
Two 'n' eight	State (nervous)

U

| Uncle Dick | Sick |
| Uncle Ned | Bed |

V

| Vera Lynn | Gin |

W

Weeping willow (pron. willer)	Pillow (pron. piller)
Whistle 'n' flute	Suit (clothes)
Widow's mite	Light
Wilkie Bards	Cards (playing)

Y

Yorkshire Tyke	Mike (Microphone)
You 'n' me	Tea

Glossary

English — Cockney

A

Alone	{Tod Sloane {Jack Jones
Arm	Chalk Farm

B

Bad	Sorry 'n' sad
Baker	Long Acre
Banana	Gertie Gitana
Bank	Joe Tank
Bar (pub)	{Bazaar {Near 'n' far
Barber	Dover Harbour
Barrow **(pron. Barrer)**	Cock sparrow (pron. sparrer)
Basin	Charley Mason
Bed	Uncle Ned
Beer	Pig's ear

Believe	Adam 'n' Eve
Belly	Derby Kelly
Bike (Bicycle)	Dirty Tyke Clever Mike
Bill (account)	Jack 'n' Jill Beecham's pill
Bird	Richard the Third
Bitter (beer)	Apple fritter
Blow	Rotten Row
Boil	Conan Doyle
Bombs	Derry 'n' Toms
Book	Rookery Nook Captain Cook
Boots	Daisy roots
Booze	River Ouse
Boozer (pub)	Battle cruiser
Boy	Hobbledy 'oy
Boy Scout	Brussels sprout
Braces	Epsom Races Airs 'n' graces
Brandy	Jack Dandy Fine 'n' dandy
Broke (financially)	Hearts of Oak Coals & coke
Bread	Needle 'n' thread
Broom	Bride 'n' groom

Brother	Love one another One 'n' t'other
Brush	Song o' the thrush
Bucket	Mrs. Duckett
Bug	Steam tug
Bum (buttocks)	Fife 'n' drum Tom Thumb
Bunion	Spanish onion
Bus	Trouble 'n' fuss
Butter	Roll me in the gutter Stammer 'n' stutter

C

Cadge	Coat 'n' Badge (Doggetts)
Cake	Put 'n' take Sexton Blake Give 'n' take
Candle	'Arry Randell
Cap (headgear)	Game o' nap
Car	Jam jar La-di-da
Card	Bladder o' lard
Cards (playing)	Wilkie Bards
Cash	Sausage 'n' mash Oscar Asche

Chair	{ Lion's share { Here 'n' there
Chairs	Owen Nares
Chalk	Pickled pork
Change (£.s.d.)	Kitchen range
Charlie	Oats 'n' barley
Cheese	{ Cough 'n' sneeze { Stand at ease
Cheque	Goose's neck
Chin	Gunga Din
Church	Lean 'n' lurch
Cider	Sit beside 'er
Cigar	{ Spanish guitar { Buck's Hussar
Clock	Dickory dock
Coach	Cockroach
Coat	I'm afloat
Coffee	Everton toffee
Cold	'Taters in the mould
Collar	'Oller boys 'oller
Cook	{ Rookery Nook { Babbling Brook { Give-a-guck { (pron. gook)
Copper (policeman)	{ Clod 'opper { Grass 'opper

Corner	Johnny 'Orner
Cough	Horse 'n' trough
Cousin	Baker's dozen
Covent Garden	Dolly Varden
Crook	Babbling Brook
Cry	Pipe yer eye
Cupboard	Mother 'Ubbard

D

Darts	Horses 'n' carts
Dawn	Cape 'Orn
Dead	Brahn bread
Deaf	Mutt 'n' Jeff
Dice	Rats 'n' mice
Dinner	Jim Skinner
Dog	Cherry 'og
Dog Racing	Cherries (the) (q.v. cherry 'ogs)
Dollar	Oxford scholar
Door	Rory O'More
Dozen	Country cousin
Drain	Spanish Main
Drink	{ Tumble dahn the sink { Tiddley-wink
Drunk	Elephant's trunk

E

Ear	King Lear
Early Bird	Word
Egg	Borrow 'n' beg
Engineer	Ginger beer
Eye(s)	Mince pie(s)

F

Face	{ Jem Mace Chevy Chase
Faces	Epsom Races
Facts	Brass tacks
Fag (cigarette)	'Arry Wragg
Fare (bus or train)	Grey mare
Farthing (pron. farden)	Dolly Varden
Feet	Plates o' meat
Fiddle	Hi-diddle-diddle
Fight	Read 'n' write
File (tool)	Duke of Argyll
Finger(s)	Long(s) & Linger(s)
Fire	{ Jeremiah Anna Maria
Fish	Lilian Gish

Fist	Oliver Twist
Five (£5)	Beehive
Fiver (£5 note)	Lady Godiva
Flicks (cinema)	Box o' tricks
Floor	Rory O'More
Flowers	April showers 'Appy arf hours Early hours
Flutter (a bet)	Grumble & Mutter
Flying Squad (Police)	Sweeney Todd
Fork	Duke o' York

G

Garden	Dolly Varden
Ghost	Pillar & post
Gin	Needle 'n' pin Vera Lynn
Gin & Bitter (mixed) (dog's nose)	Jitter
Glass (drinking)	Hackney Marsh
Gloves	Turtle doves
Glutton	Beef or mutton
Go!	Scapa Flow
Goggle Box (TV set)	Nervo 'n' Knox

Gout	Salmon trout
Gravy	Army 'n' Navy
Guards (the) (military)	Christmas cards
Guinness (stout)	Photo finish
Guts	Newington Butts
Gutter	Bread 'n' butter

H

Hair	Barnet Fair
Half a bar (ten shillings)	Jack Tar
Half Dollar	'Arf 'n Oxford Scholar
Hands	Ramsgate sands / German bands
Hat	Tit fer tat
Head	Loaf o' bread
Heart	Raspberry tart
Hill	Jack 'n' Jill
Hole	Merry old soul
Home	Pope o' Rome
Horse	Charing Cross (pron. 'Crorse')
Host	Dripping toast / Holy Ghost

Hot	Peas in the pot
House	Cat 'n' mouse

J

Jew	Half past two Buckle me shoe Four by two Five to two
Jewellery	Tomfoolery
Joanna	Piano (pron. 'pianner')
Judge	Barnaby Rudge

K

Key	Jenny Lee
Kids (children)	Saucepan lids Gawd (God) forbids
Kip (bed or sleep)	Feather 'n' flip
Kipper	Jack the Ripper
Knife	Drum 'n' fife

L

Lamp	Sarah Gamp
Lark	Bushey Park
Late	'Arry Tate

Later	Alligator
Laugh	Cow 'n' calf
Lazy	Gert 'n' Daisy
Legs	Scotch pegs
Liar	{Dunlop tyre {Holy friar
Lid (hat)	Gawd (God) forbid
Lie (untruth)	Pork pie
Light	Widow's mite
Lights	Derby Brights
Lodger	Artful Dodger
Look	Butcher's 'ook
Lunch	Kidney punch

M

Mad	Mum 'n' Dad
Magistrate	Garden Gate
Manager	Damager (Damaging Director)
Married	{Cash 'n' carried {Cut 'n' carried
Mat	Dog 'n' cat
Match (es)	Bite(s) 'n' scratch(es)
Mate	China plate
Menu	Me 'n' you

Middle	Hi-diddle-diddle
'Mike' (microphone)	Yorkshire Tyke
Mild & Bitter (mixed beer)	Smile 'n' titter
Minute (time)	Cock linnet
Miss (a girl)	Cuddle 'n' kiss
Missus (wife)	Plates 'n' dishes
Money	Bees 'n' honey
Morning	Day's a dawning
Mother	{ Love one another { One 'n' t'other
Mouth	North 'n' South
Mug	Steam Tug
Mutton	Billy Button

N

Nark (informer)	Noah's Ark
Neck	Bushel 'n' peck
Newspaper	{ Linen draper { Skyscraper
Nice	Apples 'n' rice
Nose	I suppose

O

Old man (father)	Pot 'n' pan

On the knocker (travelling salesman)	Mozzle 'n' brocha (Yiddish)
Onions	Corns & bunions
Organ	Molly O'Morgan

P

Pads (cricket)	Mums & Dads
Paper	Linen draper
Park	Noah's Ark / Light 'n' dark
Pawn	Bullock's horn
Pears	Teddy bears
Pen	Cock 'n' hen
Pepper	High stepper
Phone	Darby 'n' Joan / Molly Malone
Photo finish	Guinness
Piano (pron. pianna)	Joanna
Pickles	Harvey Nicholls
Piddle (urinate)	Jimmy Riddle
Piles (haemorrhoids)	Farmer Giles
Pillow (pron. piller)	Weeping willow (pron. willer)

Pinch (steal)	'Arf inch
Pipe (smoker's)	Cherry ripe
Pitch (cricket)	Hedge 'n' ditch
Plate	'Arry Tate
Pocket	Sky rocket Lucy Locket
Pony (£25)	Macaroni (a)
Pools (gambling)	April fools
Pork	Duke o' York
Potatoes (spuds)	Rosebuds
Pub	Rub-a-dub
Pump	Skip 'n' jump
Punter (racing)	Guzunter (goes under)

Q

| Quid (£1) | Saucepan lid |

R

| Races | Pair o' braces |
| Rain | France 'n' Spain |

Randy	Jack the Dandy
Rates	Garden gates
Rent	Duke o' Kent Burton-on-Trent
Rice	Three blind mice
Road	Frog 'n' toad
Room	Birch broom
Rotten	Reels o' cotton
Row (an altercation)	Bull 'n' cow
Rum	Tom Thumb Finger & thumb

S

Sack (dismissal)	Last card in the pack Tin tack
Saloon (bar)	Balloon
Saveloy (sausage)	Girl 'n' boy
Say so	Cocoa Tea 'n' cocoa
Scotch (whisky)	Pimple 'n' Blotch Gold watch
Sense	Eighteen pence
Serpentine (Kensington Gardens) ('Serps')	Turpentine (shortened to 'turps')

Shandy	Mahatma Gandhi
Shave	Dig in the grave
Sherry	Londonderry
Shilling (piece)	Thomas Tilling
Shirt	Dicky dirt
Shoes	Canoes Ps & Qs
Shop	Lollipop
Shovel	Lord Lovell
Sick	Uncle Dick
Silk	Cat's milk
Silly	Piccadilly Daffadown-dilly
Sister	Skin 'n' blister Black man kissed 'er
Six (Bingo)	Chop Sticks
Sixty-six (Bingo)	Clickety-click
Skint (stony broke)	Boracic lint
Sky	Apple Pie
Sleep	Bo-Peep
Slippers	Pair o' kippers
Smoke	Laugh 'n' joke
Sneeze	Bread & cheese
Soap	Cape o' good 'Ope Band of 'Ope

Socks	Almond Rocks
Son	⎧ Penny bun ⎨ Currant bun ⎩ Bath bun
Song	Ding dong
Soup	Loop the loop
Sovereign **(pron. Sovrin)**	Jimmy O'Goblin
Sparrows **(pron. sparrers)**	Bows 'n' Arrows (pron. arrers)
Spoon	Blue moon
Spuds (potatoes)	Rosebuds
Stage (theatre)	Greengage
Stairs	Apples 'n' pears
State (nervous)	⎰ Two 'n' eight ⎱ 'Arry Tate
Steak	Joe Blake
Stew	'Ow d'yer do
Stink	Pen 'n' ink
Stool	April fool
Stout (beverage)	In 'n' out
Street	Field o' wheat
Sub. (on a/c wages)	Rhubarb (pron. rubub)
Suit (clothes)	Whistle 'n' flute
Sun	Bath bun

Supper	Tommy Tupper
Swear	Lord Mayor
Sydney	Steak 'n' kidney

T

Table	Cain 'n' Abel
Tailor	Sinbad the sailor
Tanner (6d. piece)	Sprazey Anna Lord o' the Manor
Tap (dance)	Cellar flap
Tea	Rosy Lee You 'n' me
Teeth	'Ampstead 'Eath
Telephone	Molly Malone
Telly (TV set)	Marie Correlli Custard 'n' jelly
Ten pounds (£10)	Cock 'n' hen
Thief	Tea leaf
Ticket	Bat 'n' wicket
Tie	Peckham Rye
Tight (tipsy)	Isle o' Wight
Till (cash)	Jack 'n' Jill
Time	Bird lime
Toast (bread)	Holy Ghost

Toes	These and those
Tongue	Brewer's bung
Tools	April fools
Toss up (pron. torse up)	Iron horse
Train (railway)	Struggle 'n' strain
Tram	Bread 'n' jam / Baa-lamb / Plate o' ham
Trousers	Round the 'ouses
True	Eyes o' blue / Irish stew
Twenty-two (Bingo)	Dinky-do

U

| Umbrella | Cousin Ella |
| Undertaker | Overcoat maker |

V

| Vest | East 'n' West |
| Voice | Hobson's choice |

W

Wages	Greengages Rock of ages
Waistcoat **(pron. Weskit)**	Jim Prescott (pron. Preskit)
Waiter	Baked potato (pron. potater) Cold potato (pron. potater)
Walk	Ball o' chalk
Warmer	Daisy Dormer
Wash	Lemon squash
Watch (timepiece)	Gordon 'n' Gotch
Water	Fisherman's daughter
Whisky	Bright 'n' frisky Gay 'n' frisky
Wife	Trouble & strife
Window **(pron. winder)**	Burnt cinder
Wine	Rise 'n' shine
Winning post **(race course)**	Holy ghost
Word	Dicky bird Early bird

A Few Indelicacies

THERE ARE certain words we have omitted from the main text (a) because of our own pure-mindedness, (b) because of the refined nature of our readership and (c) because you can get locked up for printing words like that.

Seriously, there are words in Rhyming Slang whose English translation is a bit hair-curling. Nevertheless these words are used and ought not to be omitted from a reference work such as this.

So here we give the Cockney. The English translation you can – if you are so inclined – supply yourself.

Long Version	*Short Version*
All forlorn	Allfor
Almond Rock	Almond
Alphonse	Alphonse
Bolt the door	Bolt
Bottle and glass	Bottle
Braces & Bits	Braces
Brighton Pier	Brighton
Bristol Cities	Bristols

Charley Ronce	Charley
Coachman-on-the-box	Coachman
Cobbler's awls	Cobblers
Colleen Bawn	Colleen
Cuddled & kissed	Cuddled
Early morn	Early
Elephant & Castle	Elephant
Fish & Shrimp	Fish
Goose & duck	Goose
Grumble & Grunt	Grumble
Hampton Wick	Hampton
Hit & Miss	Hit
Joe Ronce	Joe
Khyber Pass	Khyber
King Lear	King
My word	My
Orchestra Stalls	Orchestras
Pony & trap	Pony
Richard the Third	Richard
Rugger ball	Rugger
Tom Tit	Tom

Made and Printed in Great Britain
by C. Nicholls & Company Ltd.